ALICE WATERS
COOKS UP A
FOOD
Revolution

CHEZ
Panisse

For Clementine, Peter, and Viola —D. S.

For my son, Sam, who traveled the world
with us and ate everything —J. H.

SIMON & SCHUSTER BOOKS FOR YOUNG READERS
An imprint of Simon & Schuster Children's Publishing Division
1230 Avenue of the Americas, New York, New York 10020
Text © 2022 by Diane Stanley
Illustrations © 2022 by Jessie Hartland
Book design by Lucy Ruth Cummins © 2022 by Simon & Schuster, Inc.
SIMON & SCHUSTER BOOKS FOR YOUNG READERS and related marks are trademarks of Simon & Schuster, Inc.
For information about special discounts for bulk purchases, please contact
Simon & Schuster Special Sales at 1-866-506-1949 or business@simonandschuster.com.
The Simon & Schuster Speakers Bureau can bring authors to your live event. For more information or
to book an event, contact the Simon & Schuster Speakers Bureau at 1-866-248-3049
or visit our website at www.simonspeakers.com.
The text for this book was set in Tox Typewriter.
The illustrations for this book were rendered in gouache.
Manufactured in China
0723 SCP
2 4 6 8 10 9 7 5 3
Library of Congress Cataloging-in-Publication Data
Names: Stanley, Diane, author. | Hartland, Jessie, illustrator.
Title: Alice Waters cooks up a food revolution / written by Diane Stanley ; illustrated by Jessie Hartland.
Description: Frist edition. | New York : A Paula Wiseman Book, [2022] | Includes bibliographical references. | Audience: Ages 4-8 | Audience: Grades 2-3 | Summary:
"The delicious story of pioneering chef Alice Waters who changed the way America eats and kickstarted the organic food movement. A pioneer of the slow and organic food
movements, she is also known for creating Edible Schoolyard, a project that involves kids in the growing of their own food"—Provided by publisher.
Identifiers: LCCN 2021009205 (print) | LCCN 2021009206 (ebook) | ISBN 9781534461406 (hardcover) | ISBN 9781534461413 (ebook)
Subjects: LCSH: Waters, Alice—Juvenile literature. | Natural foods—Juvenile literature. | Restaurateurs—United States—Biography—Juvenile literature. | Women
cooks—United States—Biography—Juvenile literature.
Classification: LCC TX910.5.W38 S73 2022 (print) | LCC TX910.5.W38 (ebook) | DDC 647.95092 [B]—dc23
LC record available at https://lccn.loc.gov/2021009205
LC ebook record available at https://lccn.loc.gov/2021009206

local

ALICE WATERS
COOKS UP A
FOOD
Revolution

organic

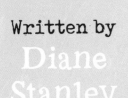

Written by
Diane Stanley

Illustrated by
Jessie Hartland

fresh!

Edible Schoolyard

A PAULA WISEMAN BOOK

NEW YORK   LONDON   TORONTO   SYDNEY   NEW DELHI

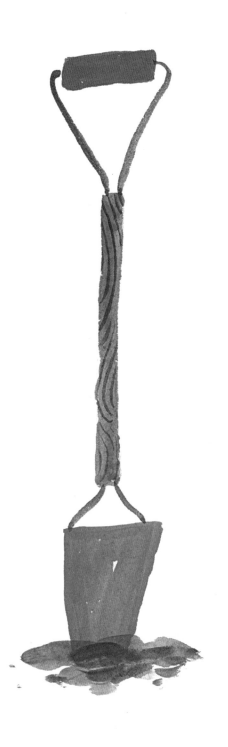

The year is 1948.
The place, an old house
in Chatham, New Jersey.
Behind the house is a
garden, and in the garden
there's a strawberry
patch, and in the
strawberry patch is a
little girl.

Her name is Alice Waters. She is picking the berries, fat and sweet, at the very peak of their flavor. The taste thrills her to the bone. She will remember it for the rest of her life.

All summer, her family eats from the garden—
asparagus, lettuce, corn, tomatoes, peppers,
strawberries, cherries, and apples.
Nothing is ever picked till it's
ripe, and they eat it that very
same day.

But when summer turns to fall, the garden goes to sleep. Then their dinners shift to "convenience food"—processed in factories, then packaged, frozen, or canned.

It's modern!

It's easy!

It's what America wants! But it doesn't taste the same.

FRANCE.

For her first French meal she goes to

a little café and orders a bowl of soup.

It's the cheapest thing on the menu,

but the taste is amazing.

IT'S THE BEST! SOUP! EVER!

The next morning she goes to a bakery and buys a baguette,

still warm from the oven. She eats it with fresh-made apricot jam.

IT'S THE BEST! BREAKFAST! EVER!

Then she tastes the crepes, cooked to order at an outdoor stand and filled with whatever she wants. She tastes delicious stews, wonderful fish, and life-changing salads.

All of them are THE BEST! EVER! And Alice knows why: because in France, all the ingredients are fresh.

Back in Berkeley for her last year of college, Alice does
everything the French way. She goes to French movies.

She reads French cookbooks and watches Julia Child's TV show, *The French Chef.*

She makes fancy French dinners for her friends. They sit around her table for hours, the way French people do, enjoying the food, friendship, and conversation.

Alice graduates from college with no plan for what to do next. Her favorite thing is French cooking, but that's not a job. It would be if she owned a restaurant, but she doesn't have the money or the experience. So instead, she works at this and that. None of it feels right.

One day she sees an old house for sale. It's kind of a mess, but she could fix it up. And it would be the perfect place for a restaurant. Like a French grandmother's house—warm and comfortable, with flowers on the tables, soft light streaming through the windows, wonderful smells drifting out of the kitchen.

Her restaurant is meant to be!

Alice borrows money from her parents and friends— et voilà!— she has the house.

Then her friends (who are now her business partners) pitch in to help.

She names
her restaurant
Chez Panisse
("Panisse's
house") after
a character in
her favorite
old French
movie.

Alice decides she won't be the chef, at least for now. She'd rather be the boss, the "Decider-in-Chief," involved in everything at Chez Panisse.

And this is what the Boss decides:

First, they'll serve a single set menu every night—with no choice!—the way she'd cook for her friends at home.

Second, the menu will be different every day.

And finally, they will use only the freshest local ingredients.

Nobody at Chez Panisse has ever run a restaurant. None of them has been to cooking school. They're artists, philosophers, filmmakers, and poets, with no clue how things are usually done in restaurant kitchens.

So they're slow and inefficient, just doing their best,

wanting every dish to be perfect, no matter how long it takes.

On opening night, with a long line of customers standing outside, they can't cook and serve the food fast enough.

At the end of the evening, with people still waiting,
Alice has to go out and apologize: Sorry! They've run out of food.

But that's okay.

They can learn, they'll do better next time, because they believe in what they're doing.

And they're so happy doing it that some nights, after the
customers have gone, the Chez Panisse family clears the floor,
cranks up some rock 'n' roll, and dances late into the night.

Alice starts holding special events at Chez Panisse.

On Bastille Day (a French national holiday) they have a grand

banquet with garlic in each of the nine courses.

And then there's the bet between two of Alice's movie-director friends, Werner Herzog and Errol Morris. Herzog bet Morris that he'd never finish his movie. "If you do," Herzog swore, "I'll eat my shoe!" Now Morris has finished the film, and Herzog has to eat his shoe.

Alice helps him cook it at Chez Panisse. They boil it for hours in duck fat, flavored with garlic and herbs. But it's still as "tough as shoe leather."

Herzog does his best anyway. He cuts it into tiny pieces,
then chews the tiny pieces while the guests cheer and applaud.

The restaurant is a success now, but Alice still isn't satisfied.

She can't seem to find the beautiful, fresh ingredients she
remembers from her childhood and her time in France.

That's because the way food is grown has been changing. Family farms are giving way to giant "agribusinesses," run for efficiency and profit, not taste.

So Alice drives all over Northern California searching for small farms,
ranches, and dairies where things are still done the old-fashioned way.

One by one, she finds them. Then she arranges to buy whatever they produce.

Finally Chez Panisse can cook in the true French way: using ingredients that are local, fresh, and organic, grown with care and patience, picked at the peak of their flavor. And it's the BEST! FOOD! EVER!

Alice and her restaurant are world famous. But while she was busy thrilling diners, gathering headlines, and winning awards, she was quietly starting a food revolution. Her vision and her passion for natural, fresh, healthy food has changed the way people everywhere—from home cooks to great restaurant chefs—think about food.

Small, traditional farms and ranches are making a comeback now. Farmers markets are popping up everywhere. Grocery stores are beginning to sell healthy, organic foods and buy directly from local farmers.

Because more and more, that's what people want. It's healthier, it's good for the earth, and it tastes better.

Thanks to Alice Waters, a new generation of children can experience the taste of a strawberry (or peach, or tomato)

that is perfectly ripe and so delicious, they will remember it for the rest of their lives.

ALICE AND HER DELICIOUS REVOLUTION

Chez Panisse is more than just a restaurant. It's a living example of great food traditions reaching back into our past. Until modern times people ate fruits and vegetables that were grown nearby, harvested at the peak of their flavor. Everyone ate according to the seasons, from the first spring greens through the rich abundance of summer, then into the fall with apples, pumpkins, and potatoes, until it came time to preserve their bounty to carry them through the winter.

All farms were organic, their soils enriched naturally. Animals raised for meat, milk, cheese, and eggs roamed freely in pastures and yards. People cooked and ate their meals at home, making everything from scratch. Families sat down to share their meals together.

Alice grew up that way. Her family didn't have a lot of money. But they had a garden that fed them beautiful, healthy food all summer long. And it was so fresh and delicious, it didn't take a lot of work to turn it into a meal.

Since then the world has moved on—to fast food; processed food; food eaten hastily in cars or at office desks; food grown with chemicals and hormones; food that gets its taste from artificial flavorings, sugar, salt, and fat; food grown in ways that harm the land and water; food grown and picked by people who are ill-treated and underfed; food that is making people sick.

Alice found these changes alarming. So she used her fame to start a national conversation that quickly spread and continues to this day. Thanks to Alice Waters, more and more people are planting gardens and visiting farmers markets, enjoying food that's fresh, local, organic, healthy, and delicious. Food grown in a way that enriches the earth instead of depleting and polluting it. Food cooked and eaten at home, once again bringing families together around a table.

THE EDIBLE SCHOOLYARD

For almost twenty-five years, on her way to and from the restaurant, Alice passed the Martin Luther King Jr. Middle School in Berkeley, California. The campus consisted of an assortment of old concrete buildings with peeling paint, broken windows, and graffiti defacing the walls, standing grimly in a barren sea of asphalt. It seemed a sad place for children to learn. One day Alice decided to do something about it.

First, she had to convince the principal that her idea could really work. Then she talked to the teachers, parents, children, and neighbors. When everyone was finally willing to give the plan a try, she created a foundation to pay for it.

Heavy machines arrived to haul off long-abandoned portable classrooms and rip up an acre of asphalt. The children helped clear away rocks, then they scattered seeds for a "cover crop" to enrich the soil over the summer. Soon they would be ready to plant a real garden—their garden.

Alice called it the Edible Schoolyard, because the garden was meant to act as a new kind of classroom, where science students could learn firsthand how plants use photosynthesis to turn sunlight into food, the importance of bees and worms, and the way all living creatures affect one another. Humanities teachers could use it to show how people lived in the past, planting and harvesting according to the seasons. Like their Neolithic ancestors, students could harvest grain they'd grown, grind it by hand into flour, then use it to make loaves of delicious bread, cooked in a wood-fired oven.

Each year brought something new. They reopened the school's ancient kitchen, built in 1921, turning it into a cheerful place where the children learned to cook the food they had grown, then sat together at a long table to enjoy a delicious meal. They built a chicken coop and brought in hens to lay eggs. They planted fruit trees and olive trees and cured their own olives. They learned by doing, by using their hands, their minds, and their senses.

Alice's Edible Schoolyard idea has grown into a network of over five thousand school garden projects in the United States and seventy-five other countries where, as Alice put it, children "come to understand the cycle of life, from seed to table and back again," learning "the relationship between the health of our bodies, our communities, and the natural world."

TIMELINE

1944 (April 28): Alice Waters is born in Chatham Borough, New Jersey

1965–66: Alice, while a student at the University of California, Berkeley, spends her junior year studying in France

1967: Alice graduates from Berkeley with a degree in French cultural studies

1968–69: Alice earns a teaching certificate at the Montessori Centre International in London and briefly works at a Montessori school in Berkeley

1971: Alice (together with her friend, film producer Paul Aratow) opens Chez Panisse

1983: Alice's daughter, Fanny, is born

1995-96: Alice establishes the Edible Schoolyard at the Martin Luther King Jr. Middle School in Berkeley and starts the Chez Panisse Foundation

2001: *Gourmet* magazine names Chez Panisse the Best Restaurant in America

2004: Alice helps develop the School Lunch Initiative for the Berkeley Unified School District

2008: Alice receives Harvard Medical School's Global Environmental Citizen Award

2010: Alice is inducted into the French Legion of Honor

2015: Alice is awarded the National Humanities Medal by President Barack Obama

2021: Chez Panisse celebrates its fiftieth anniversary

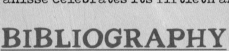

BIBLIOGRAPHY

Bertolli, Paul, and Waters, Alice. *Chez Panisse Cooking.* New York: Random House, 1988.

*Briggs Martin, Jacqueline. *Alice Waters and the Trip to Delicious.* Food Heroes series. Illustrated by Hayelin Choi and with an afterword by Alice Waters. San Francisco: Readers to Eaters, 2014

McNamee, Thomas. *Alice Waters and Chez Panisse: The Romantic, Impractical, Often Eccentric, Ultimately Brilliant Making of a Food Revolution.* New York: Penguin Books, 2007.

Waters, Alice. *Coming to My Senses: The Making of a Counterculture Cook.* New York: Clarkson Potter/Publishers, 2017.

*Waters, Alice, with Bob Carrau. *Fanny in France: Travel Adventures of a Chef's Daughter, with Recipes.* Illustrated by Ann Arnold. New York: Viking, 2016.

*Waters, Alice, with Bob Carrau and Patricia Curtan. *Fanny at Chez Panisse: A Child's Restaurant Adventure with 46 Recipes.* Illustrated by Ann Arnold. New York: HarperCollins, 1992.

Waters, Alice, with Patricia Curtan, Kelsie Kerr, and Fritz Streiff. *The Art of Simple Food: Notes, Lessons, and Recipes from a Delicious Revolution.* Illustrated by Patricia Curtan. New York: Clarkson Potter/Publishers, 2007.

*Waters, Alice, with Daniel Duane. *Edible Schoolyard: A Universal Idea.* Photographs by David Liittschwager. San Francisco: Chronicle Books, 2008.

*Denotes books for young readers.